Contents

Acknowledgements
Text by W. E. Lamb. Photograph on page 3 courtesy of Townsend Croquet Limited; all other photographs by Peter Alvey.
Illustrations by Tim Bairstow of Taurus Graphics.

Notes This book describes the British style of croquet. If you are interested in learning the slightly different American rules of play, please consult *Croquet* by Steven Boga, published by Stackpole Books.

Throughout the book players are referred to individually as 'he'. This should, of course, be taken to mean 'he or she' where appropriate.

The court and equipment

A full-size croquet court measures 35 yards × 28 yards and is bounded by a white line (measurements are usually in imperial units; a metric conversion table is given on p. 42). The boundaries are named after the points of the compass for convenience when describing the game. This is quite arbitrary and bears no relation to the actual geographic orientation of the court. One yard inside the boundaries and running parallel to them are the yard-lines, but these are not marked out. The space between the boundary and the yard-line is known as the yard-line area.

The points where the yard-lines intersect are called the corner spots and the small square enclosed by the yard-lines and the boundary lines at each corner is the corner square. The corners of the court – I, II, III, IV – are named after the hoops – 1, 2, 3 and 4 – to which they are adjacent. There are two baulk-lines, from which play starts, which run

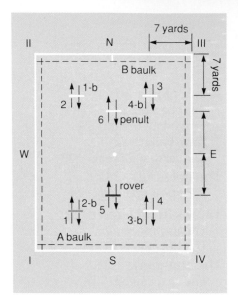

▲ *Fig. 1 The croquet court*

along the North and South yard-lines from corner III and corner I respectively to the centre of each yard-line.

Variations are allowed and beginners are strongly advised to learn, to practise and to play on a smaller court, at least until they become proficient. Short croquet (*see* p. 35) is played on courts measuring 24 yards × 16 yards.

The surface of the court should be flat and level, and the grass should be cut short enough to allow the balls to roll easily. A cut of $\frac{1}{4}''$ is usually sufficient, although for top class play the grass is cut shorter.

Court equipment

1 One peg, $1\frac{1}{2}''$ diameter, 18" high above the ground and painted white to a height of at least 6" above the ground.

2 Six hoops, $3\frac{3}{4}''$ inside measurement, 12" high above the ground, painted white. The first hoop (hoop 1) has a blue top and the last hoop (rover) has a red top.

3 Four balls coloured blue, black, red, yellow; diameter $3\frac{5}{8}''$, weight 1 lb.

4 Four spring clips coloured as the balls.

5 Mallets (*see* later).

In addition, four corner flags and eight corner pegs may be used. A check fence to halt the progress of balls struck out of court is useful.

When play is at a club, all of the above equipment will be supplied by the club for the benefit of its members, although members will usually be expected to buy their own mallet.

Lay-out of the court
(*see* fig. 1)

1   The peg is placed upright in the centre of the court.

2   Hoops 1 to 4 are set near their respective corners I to IV so that their centres are 7 yards in court from the adjacent boundaries. Hoop 1 has a blue top. Of the two remaining hoops, the one with the red top (rover) is set 7 yards to the south of the peg and the other is set 7 yards to the north of the peg. All hoops are set parallel to each other, with their openings facing south–north.

The hoops are called 1 to 6 on the

A complete croquet set: (1) peg, (2) six hoops, (3) four balls, (4) four spring clips, (5) eight corner pegs, (6) four corner flags, (7) rover hoop, (8) four mallets ▶

first circuit, and 1-back to 4-back, penult and rover on the second or reverse circuit.

3   A clip corresponding in colour with the ball is placed on the hoop which that ball has to run next. The clip is placed on the crown of the hoop for hoops 1 to 6 and on an upright for hoops 1-back to rover.

4   Where flags and corner pegs are used, a coloured flag – blue, red, black and yellow – is placed in corners I to IV respectively, and a peg is placed on the boundary 1 yard from each corner.

Mallets

Most players play with a mallet weight of about 3 lb plus or minus a couple of ounces. Many older mallets are considerably heavier and mallets which may have constituted part of a garden croquet set may be very much lighter. The head may be circular or square in cross section and will usually be about 9" in length, although longer heads are becoming more fashionable. It is made of wood or any other material which does not confer a playing advantage

compared with wood. The shaft may be of wood (usually hickory or ash), metal or fibreglass or other plastic material. Its length is usually about 36", but this may vary according to the stature and grip of the player.

If you join a club, you will normally be allowed to use a club mallet during your first season. Use this opportunity to try as many different mallets of various weights and lengths as possible. Which mallet you eventually choose will be conditioned by your own build and the type of grip and swing you adopt.

Clothing

It is always compulsory at clubs to wear flat-soled shoes to avoid damage to the court surface. All other clothing is left to the choice of the individual, but whites are normally worn at tournaments and club matches. Clothing should not restrict or impede the swing of the mallet. Rain does not stop play, so it is advisable to take some wet weather clothing such as a waterproof jacket and trousers or skirt.

The object of the game

The contestants

The game is played between two sides and can take the form of singles or doubles. Each side has two balls: black and blue always play together on one side against red and yellow on the other side. Thus in singles play, each player has two balls; in doubles play, each side has two balls and the partners on each side must decide which player will play with which ball.

Each side plays alternate turns. At the start of the turn the side to play has the choice of playing that turn with either of its two balls; once chosen, the same ball must be played throughout the turn. The other ball of that side is known as the partner ball. In doubles, once the ball to be played has been chosen, it must be played by the correct player of the side as decided at the start of the game.

The play

The object of the game is for a side to get both its balls through all six hoops in the prescribed order in each direction and then to hit the peg before the other side can do so. A point is scored for each hoop run and for hitting the peg. A full game therefore consists of 26 points – 12 hoop points and one peg point for each ball.

The game starts with the four balls being played on to the court in the first four turns. A player may play his ball on to the court from anywhere along either baulk-line.

In order to shorten the game, a course of 22 points, 18 points or 14 points may be played.

● 22 points: both balls start at hoop 3.
● 18 points: both balls start at hoop 5. Alternatively, for singles play only, one ball starts at hoop 1, the other at 3-back.
● 14 points: the course is the first six hoops in one direction only, then the peg with both balls.

Whilst it would be possible for a game of croquet to consist of turns with only a single stroke in each turn, progress would be slow. The real object is to make a break of several points by using the permitted strokes in each turn. Each successful stroke played entitles the player to a further stroke. These strokes are described below.

Single-ball strokes

At the start of each turn the player must strike the chosen ball and either cause it to run, i.e. to pass through, its next hoop in order or to roquet, i.e. hit, one of the three remaining balls to gain a further stroke.

Croquet strokes

When the player's ball roquets one of the other balls, the former is picked up – it is known as a ball in hand – and is placed in contact with the roqueted ball. The player's ball is then struck again, causing both balls to move. This is known as taking croquet and the previously roqueted ball becomes the croqueted ball. (This may seem confusing at first, but the terminology is rapidly picked up.)

Continuation strokes

A continuation stroke is a single-ball stroke played after a croquet stroke or after a hoop has been run.

During a turn a player may roquet each of the three other balls only once between scoring points by running a hoop. After a hoop has been run, the player is entitled to roquet each of the other balls once again.

A turn therefore carries on with a succession of single-ball, continuation and croquet strokes. It usually comes to an end when a single-ball stroke fails to make a roquet or run a hoop. A skilful player can use this succession of strokes to make an all-round break, i.e. score all 12 points by running all the hoops in order, with his ball, and he may even score some points for his partner ball by causing it to run its hoops in order.

Grip, style and stance

It is most important that you feel comfortable with the style, stance and grip you choose to use. You should also be able to swing the mallet freely with a full backswing, in order to hit a ball easily the full length of the court. Let the mallet do the work is a good maxim.

The grip

There are three main ways of gripping the mallet, known as the Standard, Irish and Solomon grips.

Standard grip

The upper hand, usually the left hand for a right-handed player, grips the mallet with the fingers curled around the shaft and with the knuckles pointing forwards. The lower hand grips with the palm of the hand behind the shaft. It is usually better to have the hands close together, so that they share the work of swinging the mallet. Some players find this rather unwieldy and prefer to keep the hands apart.

Irish grip

With the Irish grip both the upper and lower hands grip the shaft with the palms either behind or to the side. Some players like to extend the index finger of the upper hand along the shaft and to

overlap this finger with the fingers of the lower hand. The grip is usually a little lower down the shaft of the mallet. (Players using the Irish grip often play with a shorter-shafted mallet.)

Grips: standard (left), Irish (centre) and Solomon (right)

mallet. This grips allows a very free swing of the mallet.

Each of the three grips has its adherents, but there is no clear-cut advantage to any one of them. Beginners should adopt whichever grip feels most natural and comfortable to them. If the grip is not comfortable, repeated swinging of the mallet may lead to repetitive strain injury.

Style and stance

Centre style

In this style the mallet is swung between the feet and legs. The head is then naturally over the line of the swing. The feet should be placed parallel to the line of the swing and preferably side by side about 6″ to 9″ apart, so that the body is square to this line. (There is a natural tendency for beginners to stand with their feet splayed apart, for fear that they may hit their ankles with the mallet on the swing. This fear is quite groundless, as the mallet actually swings below the level of the ankles, and a misdirected swing will merely brush against the foot.) The weight should be

Solomon grip

Both hands curl round the mallet shaft with the knuckles in front. The hands are usually together at the top of the

▲ *Centre style*

evenly distributed between the feet.

If you feel that you are beginning to lose your balance when you are swinging the mallet, particularly with a full backswing, then try a stance with one foot drawn back a little. Be careful, however, not to draw back the corresponding hip and shoulder, or you will affect the line of the swing.

The swing is mainly from the shoulders, i.e. the mallet and the arms should feel as if they are swinging as one unit, and it is necessary to bend forwards from the waist to allow the hands and arms sufficient room to move. Too upright a stance will inhibit this movement.

Side style

In this style the mallet is swung to the side of the feet and the body. The feet are usually placed with one foot in front of the other and with the weight mainly on the forward foot. The shoulders and hips should remain square to the line of aim. The grip is usually the Standard grip, with the hands separated.

As the body no longer impedes the movement of the lower hand, the stance can be more upright and commends itself to elderly players. Side-style players often play with a longer-shafted mallet. However, this style is rarely used amongst top-class players.

Side style ▶

▲ *The backswing*

▲ *Impact*

◀ *The follow-through*

9

Single-ball strokes

Before going on to the play and tactics necessary to win a game of croquet, the player must learn how to strike the ball accurately and what sort of strokes are necessary to get it round the course to the peg.

Plain hit

You may wish to send your ball to another part of the court. Even if you are not aiming to hit another ball, it will pay to select a definite aiming point. Stand back from your ball along the extension of the line joining the aiming point and the ball. Walk forwards along this line, looking towards the aiming point, until you arrive at your ball. This method, known as 'stalking' the ball, will help to get your feet and body in alignment.

When you arrive at the ball, lower your mallet so that the mallet head is just behind the ball. Look up towards your target and then down again at the ball. Swing the mallet backwards by

▲ *Stalking the ball*

pulling with the arms – remember the swing comes from the shoulders – and then move it steadily forwards, keeping your gaze fixed to the ball. Hit the ball with the centre of the mallet face when the head is parallel to the ground and follow the stroke through. Resist any temptation to look up too early to see where the ball has gone.

The swing should be smooth and unhurried, particularly at the top of the backswing. Any jerkiness will spoil the accuracy of the hit. Practise hitting your ball so that it comes to rest on a spot on the court a predetermined distance away. Vary this distance so that you can hit accurately as far as the greatest distance you need, i.e. from one corner to the diagonally opposite corner. Don't try to hit harder on the more distant shots by forcing the forward swing; instead, lengthen the backswing and try to keep the same rhythm as for gentler strokes.

Practise swinging the mallet smoothly as much as you can until it becomes a natural movement. Even if you do not have space to hit a ball at home, you can practise hitting an imaginary ball.

The roquet

Now place another ball about 3 yards away from your own ball to serve as a target. Follow the same procedure outlined for the plain hit, remembering to stalk the ball first. Swing smoothly and easily, keeping your gaze fixed on your own ball. Above all, don't look up too early – you will hear your ball hit the other one even if you do not see it!

Gradually extend the distance between the two balls until you are making the roquet at least fifty per cent of the time. Make a mental note of this distance. In a game it will be important to have a good idea of your chances of making a roquet. As you improve, your fifty/fifty distance will increase.

Confidence is very important. At first, you may be concentrating too much on the individual aspects of the swing and this can cause some tension in the muscles. Relax and let the swing be smooth. Don't let your eyes be distracted from looking at your own ball during the swing.

The roquet ▶

The rush

Place another ball about 12″ in front of your own ball: select a spot about 10 yards away on the extension of the line between the two, and strike your ball so that it hits the other ball and propels it to the selected spot. This type of roquet, where the roqueted ball comes to rest in a predetermined position, is called a *rush*.

Remember to follow the normal procedure for hitting your ball. There is an additional difficulty with the rush: because the target ball is so close, it is easy to take your eye off your own ball. If you look towards the target ball, you may actually sway forwards slightly, thus striking your own ball before the mallet head has reached the horizontal position. Striking down on the ball will squeeze it into the turf and it will jump off the turf on the rebound and hit the target ball above centre. It may even jump over the target ball!

Some players counteract this tendency by deliberately standing back an inch or two from their own ball when playing a rush. You may wish to try this if you are experiencing this difficulty,

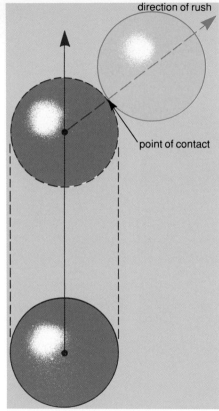

▲ *Fig. 2 The cut rush*

but it is better to keep your concentration fixed on your own ball and treat the rush as any other hit.

Gradually extend the distance between the two balls to about a yard. Beyond this separation it is difficult for beginners to rush accurately. In practice always try to rush the roqueted ball a predetermined distance.

You will soon discover that if you do not hit accurately, the roqueted ball will not travel straight ahead but will be directed to one side or the other. If your ball hits the target ball to the left of centre, that ball will be rushed to the right, and vice versa. This is the principle of the *cut rush* and it can be turned to your advantage whenever necessary. Just remember that if you want to rush the ball to the right, aim slightly to the left of centre and vice versa. You can actually select a line of aim by imagining your ball striking the target ball. The target ball will be rushed along the line joining the centres of the two balls and passing through the point of contact.

The rush can be a very important stroke in the game because it can make all the difference to the ease or difficulty of the next stroke.

Hoop running

The technique for playing your ball through the hoop – running the hoop as it is known – is just that of a normal single-ball stroke. If the ball is directly in front of the hoop, stalk it carefully, aiming for a point in the centre of the hoop. Swing gently and smoothly, keeping your eye on the ball, and follow through normally. The ball will start to roll almost as soon as it leaves the mallet and this forward spin will help it through the hoop, even if the aim is a little misdirected. In contrast, a jerky action may cause the ball to skip or slide, and it will not acquire the helpful forward spin.

Of course, more often than not, your hoop running stroke will have to be made from an angle. The technique for running angled hoops is no different from that for running straight hoops, except that the line of aim is a little different. In this case it should be such that the ball will just miss the near wire of

▲ Hoop running

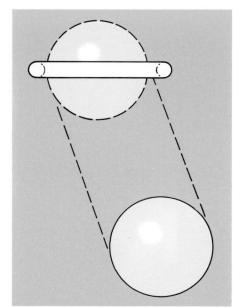

▲ Fig. 3 Running an angled hoop: aim to miss the near wire

13

the hoop and bounce off the far wire through the hoop. Any deflection off the near wire will almost inevitably result in the ball sticking in the hoop. Remember the action should be as smooth as possible and as gentle as is consistent with running the hoop in order to let the ball roll. Too many players try to bully the ball through the hoop by hitting hard and hoping for the best.

When you are in a good position to run a hoop, you should try to use just sufficient force to make the ball stop where you want it to.

▲ *Angled hoop running*

Croquet strokes

When you have made a roquet your ball becomes a ball in hand. You pick it up and put it in contact in any position you wish with the ball you have just roqueted. You then *take croquet* from that ball by striking your own ball once again with the mallet. This *croquet stroke* is unique to croquet and gives the game its name. The object of the croquet stroke is to send both balls to preselected positions.

There are many different ways of playing croquet strokes, depending on the relative distances and directions that you want the two balls to go.

The take-off

This is the easiest of the croquet strokes to play, because it is almost like a single-ball shot. It is used when you want to send your own ball to some other spot, leaving the croqueted ball almost where it lies.

To do this, place your own ball in contact with the roqueted ball so that they

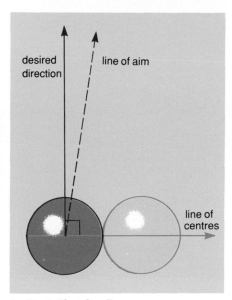

▲ *Fig. 4 The take-off*

are at right angles to the direction in which you want your ball to go. When you take your position for the stroke, you should aim in slightly towards the roqueted ball, so that it moves away slightly after impact. It is a fault not to move or shake the croqueted ball, or to hit it with your mallet. Whereas expert players can play this stroke so that the croqueted ball only shakes but does not move, it is far safer for beginners to aim in sufficiently to move the croqueted ball about one inch for every yard that their own ball travels.

Because the croqueted ball travels so little, the strength of the shot is almost the same as playing an ordinary single-ball shot. It is a great advantage to develop a good touch on this shot. A good take-off to a ball twenty yards away may leave you with a simple one-yard roquet: a poor one may leave an awkward five-yard roquet.

Straight croquet strokes

These strokes are played so that the mallet's line of swing is along the line joining the centres of the two balls in contact and thus passing through their point of contact. In this case both balls will travel along this line and the only problem is to get each ball to travel the correct distance.

The drive

The drive is hit in exactly the same way that you would hit a single ball shot, with the head of the mallet level at impact and with a normal follow-through. Naturally, you will feel more resistance at impact, because you are making two balls rather than one move. This is by far the easiest of the croquet strokes, because you are not trying to do anything special.

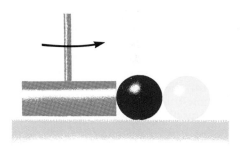

▲ *Fig. 5 The drive*

The croqueted ball will travel further than your ball, typically three to four times as far, and knowledge of this ratio is vital to all other straight croquet strokes. The actual ratio achieved depends upon the weight of the mallet, particularly the head weight, the stiffness of the shaft and the normal position

15

of the player's hands. It is worth pacing out the two distances when you first practise the drive. It will help you to visualise the relative distances the two balls travel when the drive is struck at different strengths.

The stop shot

This is the stroke to play when you want to increase the relative distances the two balls travel, i.e. to send the croqueted ball much further than your own. The shot is played most easily with a relaxed grip, with the hands well towards the top of the shaft and without a follow-through.

Many players stand back a couple of inches when addressing the ball for a

▲ *The stop shot*

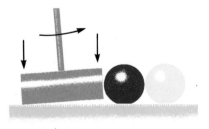
▲ *Fig. 6 The stop shot*

stop shot, thus raising the front face (toe) of the mallet head a little. On the forward swing the rear face (heel) of the mallet is grounded by pushing the mallet downwards at the moment of impact in order to prevent a follow-through. This is a very effective technique, but it does require good timing. The swing should remain smooth and care should be taken not to jab the mallet forwards.

Once you have mastered the action of the stop shot you should be able to send the croqueted ball easily six times as far as your own ball: good players can get ratios as high as 10 : 1. If you cannot get a good stop shot ratio, it may be that your mallet is too heavy.

The roll

The opposite of the stop shot, when you want to send your own ball further in relation to the croqueted ball, is the roll. Lower your grip with both hands – if you play normally with both hands together, they will have to be separated – and stand closer to the ball. You will have to bend much more from the waist and also at the knee to address the ball. It is difficult to maintain your balance in this position if your feet are side by side, so your right foot (for a right-handed player) should be withdrawn. Your weight should be mostly on your front foot, which should be parallel to the line of swing.

In this position you will be addressing

▲ *The roll*

▲ *Fig. 7 The roll*

the ball with the heel of the mallet raised and hitting your ball on the downward swing before the mallet head becomes horizontal. Whilst some follow-through is acceptable, care should be taken not to make this excessive. Pushing the back ball after the croqueted ball has departed is a fault, as is striking it twice in the same stroke.

In general, the lower your hands and the more you stand forward, the further the back ball will travel in relation to the croqueted ball. However, you should avoid playing the stroke with the lower hand at the bottom of the shaft. Not only is it a fault to touch the mallet head when playing a stroke, but it will also prevent you from playing powerfully.

17

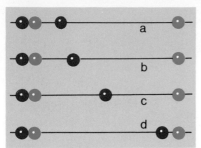

▲ *Fig. 8 Typical ratios for (a) the stop shot;*
(b) the drive; (c) the half-roll; (d) the full roll

Once the technique has been acquired, it is not a difficult stroke to play. By experimenting with hand and foot positions you will be able to control the ratio of distances travelled by both balls from a half-roll (the back ball travels half as far as the front one) to the full roll (where both balls travel the same distance).

Split croquet strokes

You will not always want to send the balls straight ahead. In fact, more often you will want to send the croqueted ball in one direction and your own ball in another.

It is quite easy to determine the direction in which the croqueted ball will travel. It travels along the line passing through the centres of the two balls and the point of contact (*see* fig. 9) and is independent of the direction in which you swing the mallet. Unfortunately there is no general rule which will tell you in all circumstances which direction your ball will take, but the following is a good approximation: the mallet's line of swing bisects the directions in which the two balls travel.

You can control the relative distance travelled by the two balls as for straight croquet strokes by playing the stroke with a stop shot, drive or roll action.

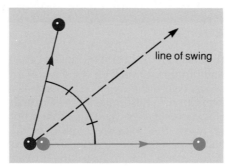

line of swing

▲ *Fig. 9 Split croquet stroke*

▲ ▼ *The split croquet stroke*

The following four steps will enable you to set up the split croquet stroke.

1 Place your ball in contact with the roqueted ball so that the line joining the centres of the two balls is pointing in the required direction.

2 Determine which direction you want your ball to go.

3 Split the angle between these two directions: this is your aiming direction and the line along which you swing the mallet.

4 Choose the kind of stroke play, i.e. stop shot, drive or roll.

With experience this will become second nature to you. The ability to play good split croquet strokes is one of the hallmarks of a good player, and a well-executed split is one of the most satisfying strokes to play.

Hoop approach

This is the term given to the croquet stroke with which you get your ball into position to go through the hoop in the next stroke. However, this is not the only objective of the hoop approach. After you have run the hoop with your ball, you will usually have to roquet one of the other balls for the turn to continue. The hoop approach should be played, therefore, in such a way that the croqueted ball may be easily roqueted after the hoop has been run and, if possible, rushed in a convenient direction.

Naturally, it is easier to get a good position to run a hoop if the hoop approach is made from a position reasonably close to it. Hoop approaches are characterised by the positions from which they are made.

Front or normal approach

This approach is made from a position in front of the hoop. Before making the

▲ *The hoop approach*

19

hoop approach, think what you want to do after running the hoop. If you want to go straight ahead, e.g. after hoops 1 or 3, you should send the croqueted ball well past the hoop with a stop shot; if you want to go sideways, e.g. after hoops 2 or 2-back, you should send the croqueted ball only a little ahead and to the appropriate side with a half roll; finally, if you want to reverse direction, e.g. after hoops 4 or 4-back, send the roqueted ball to the appropriate side and just past the hoop with a three-quarter roll. Of course, the exact stroke you play will depend on the distance to the hoop.

Side approach

If in your previous stroke you have rushed the roqueted ball to the side of the hoop, you will have to play a little split croquet stroke to croquet the other ball past the hoop and to leave your ball in a position to run the hoop. Be careful here to aim correctly and swing along this line. There is always a strong temptation to allow the swing to wander in the direction you want your ball to go; this inevitably results in your ball being too far from the hoop. You also need to allow a reasonable margin of error on

this shot. If you attempt to get too close to the hoop with your ball, you have to be very accurate.

Backward approach

If you rush the roqueted ball behind the hoop, you have to approach the hoop with a take-off, usually known in this case as a backward take-off. Place your ball in contact with the roqueted ball on the side away from the hoop, so that it will stop at a suitable point in front of the hoop, and swing towards the near wire of the hoop.

Of these three approaches the front approach is the easiest to play and you have control over the position to which the croqueted ball is sent. Many beginners like to play the backward take-off because this seems quite an easy stroke to play. However, there is no control whatsoever over the position of the croqueted ball and subsequent strokes may become harder to play.

It is a characteristic of the good croquet player that he makes a break as easy as possible by controlling the position of both balls in a hoop approach and with croquet strokes in general.

Break play

Throughout the game the aim of the player should be to 'make a break', i.e. to score more than one point in a single turn. Everyone's ambition is to reach the stage of proficiency when they can take a ball round the course from the first hoop to the last in a single turn – an all-round break. Expert players can not only do this, but can also *peel* (push) their partner ball through several of its hoops in the same turn.

Breaks are divided according to the number of balls used in making them and there are, therefore, three kinds: two-ball, three-ball and four-ball. The more balls used in a break, the more difficult it is to arrange but the easier to sustain once arranged.

Two-ball break

With the two-ball break you have only one other ball to help you. This break is naturally the easiest to 'pick up', as you have a potential two-ball break whenever you are in a position to rush a ball

◀ *Lining up a peel*

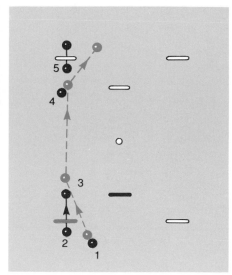

▼ *Fig. 10 Two-ball break*

to your next hoop. However, to keep the break going requires a good deal of skill (or luck).

Suppose in fig. 10 you have to run hoop 1 with your ball and have rushed a ball to it. You must now play your hoop approach stroke with great care to place the croqueted ball past the hoop to a position where it may be subsequently rushed to hoop 2. After playing the approach, you must run the hoop carefully with the right strength to obtain the rush. You must then rush the ball to hoop 2 accurately over a distance of some 20 yards.

There are three strokes in the sequence:

1 the hoop approach
2 the hoop-running stroke
3 the rush to the next hoop.

All three must be performed with accuracy in order to get position at the next hoop.

Three-ball break

With this break there are two other balls to help you. One ball, called the *pilot ball*, is handily placed by the next hoop in order; the other, called the *pioneer ball*, is waiting at the next hoop but one. The

21

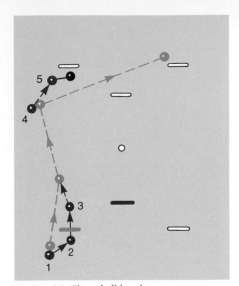

▲ *Fig. 11 Three-ball break*

pilot is there to help you negotiate the next hoop and make a roquet afterwards (*see* fig. 11). It is then sent to act as a pioneer a hoop ahead of the break, whilst your ball finishes close to the pilot (previously the pioneer) at the next hoop (*see* fig. 11).

There are five strokes in the sequence, which is repeated at each hoop. These are:

1   the roquet on the pilot for the next hoop
2   the hoop approach
3   the hoop-running stroke
4   the roquet or rush on the pilot
5   the croquet stroke sending the pilot to be a pioneer at the next hoop but one.

To sustain the break easily, the pioneers must be sent out accurately at stroke five of the sequence. To do this, the roquet or rush on the previous pilot at stroke four should be to a position which makes stroke five as easy as possible. To get a good rush at stroke four, strokes three and two must be accurate, and these in turn depend upon the accuracy of stroke one.

As long as this accuracy is maintained, then the break is not too difficult to play. When control of the break is lost, the succeeding strokes become more difficult until control is regained. For example, in fig. 11, if the pilot cannot be rushed as shown, but merely roqueted where it is, then a more diffi-

cult split croquet stroke has to be played instead of a simple straight one.

Four-ball break

With this break there are three other balls to help you. As with the three-ball break, there is a pilot at the next hoop and a pioneer at the next hoop but one. The extra ball is known as the *pivot ball* and is usually located somewhere in the vicinity of the peg. The presence of the pivot makes the break much easier to handle, although it increases the number of strokes in the sequence to seven. The strokes are (*see* fig. 12):

1   the roquet on the pilot for the next hoop
2   the hoop approach
3   the hoop-running stroke
4   the roquet or rush on the pilot
5   the croquet stroke sending the pilot to be a pioneer at the next hoop but one; the player's ball finishes close to the pivot
6   the roquet on the pivot
7   the croquet stroke (usually a take-off) to send the player's ball to the pilot at the next hoop.

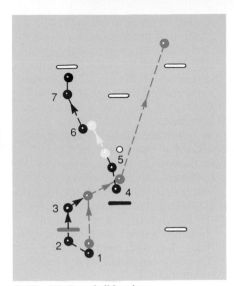

▲ *Fig. 12 Four-ball break*

There are several advantages to the four-ball break in comparison with the two-ball and three-ball breaks:

● all the strokes are relatively short and straight, and are consequently easier

● it does not matter so much if you don't get a rush on the pilot after making a hoop

● if you don't succeed in getting a good pioneer at stroke five, there is still a chance to send the pivot to act as the pioneer.

Converting a break

Because a four-ball break is easier to play, you should always try to convert any other break upwards until it becomes a four-ball break. A two-ball break may be converted into a three-ball break if there is another ball in court from the yard-line by rushing the pilot towards it after making a hoop. The next croquet stroke puts the old pilot as a pioneer at the next hoop but one, leaving a rush on the third ball to the next hoop (*see* fig. 13).

During a three-ball break the fourth ball is easiest to pick up from a corner or a boundary as play approaches the hoop nearest to it. Fig. 14 shows the continuation of the previous position with yellow in corner III. After hoop 2 black is rushed further in court and red takes off to and roquets yellow. On the following croquet stroke yellow is sent as a pioneer to hoop 4, with red finishing close to the pilot, blue, at hoop 3.

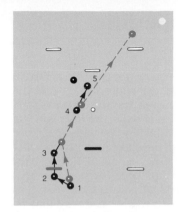

▲ *Fig. 13 Two-ball to three-ball break*
▼ *Fig. 14 Three-ball to four-ball break*

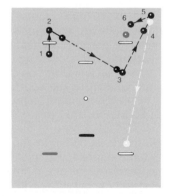

23

The opening

At the start of the game a coin is tossed, normally by the better player, and the winner of the toss has the choice of start or the choice of balls; the loser has the choice not taken by the winner. Choice of start gives the opportunity to play first or to make the opponent do so. With experienced players there is no real advantage to be gained by choosing to play first; with weaker players it may be slightly better to do so (but *see* p. 30 for handicap play).

There should be no advantage to playing with any particular colours, provided that the balls are reasonably matched, but many players automatically choose Red and Yellow. The first two normal turns of each side are used to play the four balls on to the court. Each ball may be played from any point on either baulk-line at the striker's choosing.

There is little point in trying to run the first hoop from A baulk: if you make the hoop, you merely score one point with little opportunity to continue with

a break; if you fail and bounce back off the wire, you present your opponent with a chance to make an easy roquet and maybe a break. The start of the game is really a contest to gain the innings and take control of the game. Most games start with the standard opening, which is described below.

Standard opening

(It may help you if you remember that 'Ray' is a mnemonic for 'Red and Yellow', and 'Bab' is a mnemonic for 'Black and Blue'.)

Let's suppose that Bab has won the toss and chosen to play first. Ray has chosen to play with Red and Yellow.

1 Bab plays a ball, say Black, from A baulk off the court on the east boundary in the vicinity of hoop 4.
2 Ray lays a *tice* with Red, i.e. plays it from A baulk to a point on the west boundary a few yards from corner 1. He does this to entice Bab to shoot at it and miss. The length of the tice will depend upon his estimate of Bab's prowess in shooting. Too long and she will ignore the tice; too short and she will probably hit.

3 Bab must now assess the position. If she thinks she can hit the tice or that Ray will probably do so, she should shoot at the tice from corner one. (This should be played sufficiently firmly so that blue will finish in or near corner II if the tice is missed.)
● If Bab hits the tice, she plays a take-off to Black, moving Red further up the court – at least to half-way. She then roquets Black and lays a rush towards the Red. It is unlikely that Ray will '*hit in*' on the fourth turn as there is no easy shot. Bab would then continue with the rush to Red, croquet Black towards hoop 2 and leave a rush on Red to hoop 1.
● If Bab declines to shoot at the tice, she should join up with Black on the east boundary.
4 Ray must now play Yellow on to the court. His options will be determined by Bab's play at turn 3 above.
● If Bab has hit the tice or declined it, Ray should shoot at Red from a position on A baulk which will leave Yellow in or near corner II, should

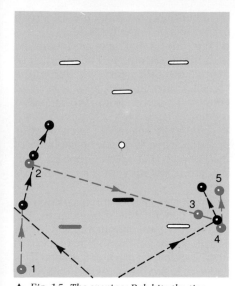

▲ *Fig. 15 The opening: Bab hits the tice*

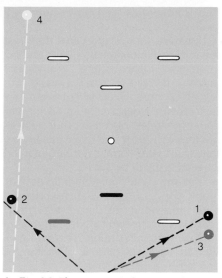

▲ *Fig. 16 The opening: Bab ignores the tice; Ray misses*

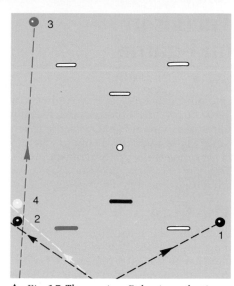

▲ *Fig. 17 The opening: Bab misses the tice; Ray misses the shot*

he miss. If he hits, he should take off with Yellow to the joined up Black and Blue, roquet one, and croquet it out a little into court, leaving a rush to hoop 1 on the other.

● If Bab has played at the tice and missed, Ray should shoot at it at an angle from A (or B) baulk. This will ensure that Red and Yellow are joined up, if he misses.

Of these possibilities the advantage goes to Bab if

● she shoots at the tice and hits; or

● if she ignores the tice and Ray misses it.

The advantage goes to Ray if

● Bab misses the tice; or

● she ignores the tice and he hits it.

The standard opening is thus nicely balanced. Each player has the opportunity to gain the advantage with a good shot or to lose it with a missed shot.

Tactics in mid-game

Like all sports croquet is a kind of war game but played, of course, in a friendly spirit and with no injury to the loser. Nevertheless, you are trying to win and to prevent your opponent from doing so. You try to turn situations to your advantage and against your opponent.

The in-player

In croquet the advantage lies with the player who has the *innings*, i.e. the player who has hit a roquet and is playing a turn of more than one stroke. He is known as the *in-player*. If you are the in-player, you must try to retain that advantage at the end of your turn. Leave the balls in such a position that your opponent will not find it easy to hit in, but you will be able to continue on your next turn. In other words, at the conclusion of your turn your balls should be *joined up*, i.e. close together, and your opponent's should be well separated both from each other and yours.

This is known as *laying up* or making a *leave*.

However, there is more to it than just separating the opponent's balls and rejoining your partner ball. You should actually try to construct a leave that will allow you to make progress on your next turn, whatever your opponent does – provided, of course, that he does not make a roquet and wrest the advantage from you. Some examples of good leaves are given below.

● Put one of the opponent balls at your next hoop as a pilot and the other at your next hoop but one as a pioneer; finish with your two balls laid up with a rush to your next hoop. This will give you an excellent chance of making a break if he misses a shot.

● If your two balls are for different hoops, leave an opponent ball at each of them as a pilot and lay up with a rush to one of them. Whichever ball your opponent moves, you will have a pilot and a good chance of a break.

● If the two hoops in the previous leave are too close together (giving your opponent a good chance to hit in), then put one of the opponent balls by one hoop and the other somewhere near the

centre of the court. Lay up with a rush to that ball or to the hoop.

● Put one of the opponent balls by your next hoop but one and the other in the middle of the court (wired from it if possible), then lay up with a rush to your next hoop from the adjacent corner.

● *Wire* your opponent's balls at your hoop, i.e. leave them one on each side of the hoop so that they cannot hit each other, and lay up with a rush towards them.

● Don't leave a favourable position for your opponent if he should hit in. For example, when constructing the leaves above, be careful not to leave an opponent ball by its partner's hoop. It is better to leave the opponent balls each by its own hoop. Whichever ball your opponent hits in with will not then have a pilot for its hoop.

● If one of the opponent balls has made a lot more hoops than the other, put that ball where it will be of most use to you in your next turn. You then 'force' the opponent to play with his forward ball, when he would probably prefer to play with the backward ball.

● If one of your balls has made many

more hoops than the other, lay up with a useful rush for the backward ball.

● Always lay up by a boundary and preferably a yard or two in from the yard-line. Then, if your opponent shoots at your balls and misses, you will be able to roquet his ball, stop it out into court and get a rush on your partner ball.

● When laying up a rush be careful not to leave your opponent with a double target.

You should be aware, when playing your turn, of your capability with the various strokes employed. Sometimes it will be necessary at the start of a turn to play one or two difficult shots in order to pick up a break. This may entail some danger of breaking down and conceding the innings to your oponent. You have to assess the reward that will come from success in comparison with the penalty that will ensue from failure. If the odds are against you, then it is time to play safe: use your turn to rearrange the balls on the court to your advantage with a view to making progress on your next turn.

This kind of risk management is an important part of the tactics of croquet, but don't take it too far. Don't become the type of player who doesn't try to make a break and does nothing but separate the opponent balls on each turn. Such players are known as 'Aunt Emmas' and are deservedly unpopular and rarely successful.

The out-player

The out-player is the player who does not have the innings. When you are the out-player pay attention to your opponent's play and wait patiently for your turn. Remember you and your opponent are joint referees of the game and you will not be able to discharge your duty if you have wandered away to talk to someone. Unobserved errors in play occur quite frequently, especially with less experienced players.

When it is your turn to play, you will be faced with two immediate decisions: which ball to play with and what to do with it.

Which ball?

● If your opponent has broken down and left one of your balls close to any other, then obviously play with it.

● If your opponent has made a good leave, play with the ball that is by your opponent's next hoop unless you have a very good chance of hitting in with the other ball. If your opponent has left each of your balls by one of his hoops, play with the one that is by the hoop of his backward ball.

● If your opponent has not made a

27

good leave and you have a free choice of ball to play with, play with the ball that will give you the best chance to make a break if you hit in.

What to do?
● If your opponent has broken down with his balls widely separated and you have no easy roquet, join up with your partner ball.
● If you have a *free shot* at any ball, i.e. one that will leave your ball in a safe position, take that shot.
● If a free shot is not available, assess the danger of shooting at and missing one of the other balls in comparison with your chance of hitting in and making a break. The danger will depend upon your opponent's skill or upon the possibility that he may take a bisque to turn the position to his advantage. If the odds seem in your favour, take the shot.
● If the odds above seem too unfavourable, play your ball to a safe position and wait for a better opportunity. The safe position will usually be in or close to a corner behind the break of your opponent's preferred ball. For example, if your opponent's backward ball is for hoop 4, then play to the third corner.

28

The·end-game

If your forward ball is for the peg and you are playing a break with your backward ball, there is little to worry about. Play with care and you should finish on that turn. Try to arrange the break so that your partner ball does not become the pioneer at rover. You then avoid the necessity of rushing it back to the peg.

However, it is usually not wise to take the forward ball to the peg if the backward ball has a lot of hoops to make. You would run the risk of having your forward ball pegged out by your opponent should you lose the innings. This would put you at a serious disadvantage, for you would have no partner ball to join up with at the end of your turn. You should only take the forward ball to the peg when you are quite certain that you will be able to finish the game in your next turn. Otherwise, you should stop at rover or possibly penult, depending on the skill of your opponent. An expert opponent would be able to peel your forward ball through rover and peg it out anyway.

The rover hoop

If you have stopped at rover with the forward ball, you may be able to peel it through with the backward ball and peg both balls out to finish the game.

Arrange the break so that your partner ball is the pioneer at rover. Take one of the opponent balls up to rover after making penult and croquet it just past and to one side of rover. Roquet or rush your partner ball in front of rover and peel it through firmly with the croquet stroke. Run rover gently with your own ball and roquet the opponent ball. Take off to get position behind your partner ball and rush it to the peg ready for the peg-out.

Don't take risks though, in trying the peel; it is far better to end the turn with a tidy leave for peg and rover than to break down with several balls around the rover hoop.

If it is not possible or advisable to peel your partner ball, take your ball to the peg and try to arrange a wired leave at rover. Otherwise, leave the opponent balls well separated and lay up with a rush to rover. If your opponent misses his last shot, rush the partner ball to

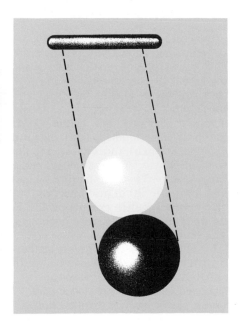

▼ *Fig. 18 The peel from a slight angle: aim to miss the near wire*

rover, and roll your partner ball slightly past rover and just to one side with the croquet stroke. Then, after making rover, you can rush the partner ball to the peg for the peg-out.

The peg-out

Only a rover ball, i.e. one that has run the rover hoop in order, may peg itself out by hitting the peg. In addition, a rover ball may peg out any other rover ball by causing it to hit the peg. In handicap play you may not peg out your own rover ball until its partner has also become a rover ball.

The idea is to peg out your partner ball with a croquet stroke and then peg out your own ball with the continuation stroke. The further the balls are from the peg, the more difficult it is to do this with certainty. You roquet your partner ball if it is close to the peg, or rush it there if it is some distance away. (Be careful not to rush it on to the peg and thereby peg it out accidentally: it

▲ *The peg-out*

29

would then be the end of your turn, as you would be unable to take croquet.)

Line the balls up carefully so that the line through their centres points to the centre of the peg. It is best to get down to do this; the lower, the better. If you look from a low position, you will see the whole of your ball and a cusp or arc of the roqueted ball. The line of sight over the tops of these two should go to the peg. An alternative method is to sight tangentially on each side past the edges of both balls. The peg should appear displaced an equal amount on each side.

Make certain that the two balls are in contact, take aim carefully with the mallet and play a normal straight drive. Hit the stroke firmly so that your ball will finish a couple of feet past the peg if it does not strike it. Of course, if your ball does hit the peg in the croquet stroke, it is pegged out as well. In general, it is better to avoid the roll stroke when attempting a peg-out, as it is far too easy to pull the croqueted ball off the line with a roll. An exception may be when the opponent balls are well separated and your balls are too far from the peg. You may then want to roll up to the peg and peg out your ball if the croqueted

ball misses. However, you will leave a last shot through the middle of the court to your opponent; a better play may be to roll both balls to a position remote from the opponent balls and leave a rush to the peg for a peg-out in your next turn.

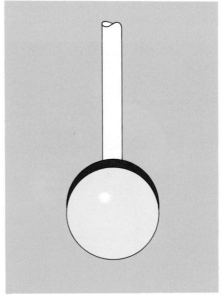
▲ Fig. 19 Lining up the peg-out

Handicaps

Croquet has an excellent handicapping system which allows players of different abilities to play a competitive game together. All players who belong to a club are given a club handicap and those who play in tournaments are given a Croquet Association (CA) handicap. The handicap takes the form of *bisques*, or extra turns allowed to the weaker player. CA handicaps may range from − 5 to 8 in intervals of a half and from 8 to 20 in unit intervals, but club handicaps often extend upwards to 24 or even 30 for complete beginners. The system works as follows.

1 In singles play one bisque (extra turn) is given to the weaker player for each unit difference of handicap between them. (In full bisque play each player receives an allocation of bisques equal to his handicap.)

2 A half-bisque is an extra turn with the restriction that no point can be scored for either side during that turn. Full bisques may not be converted into two half-bisques.

3 A bisque may be taken at the end of any turn at any time in the game.
4 The same ball must be played for the bisque turn as was used for the previous turn.

When to take a bisque

The more bisques you receive, the more important it is to take them early in the game. After all, you are then playing against a much better player and the more chances you give him, the greater the danger that he might get both his balls round and finish the game, leaving you with unused bisques. Don't be over-awed by an expert opponent: on the contrary, with a lot of bisques it is actually easier for you to play and it is a good chance for you to go on the attack and show what you can do. The 'classic' opening against a scratch or minus player is a good example.

Here one or two bisques are used to set up a four-ball break with the intention of taking it as far as possible or advisable. You have won the toss and put your opponent in (to have the first opportunity with four balls on the lawn). Your opponent has played his first ball, Red, to the east boundary opposite hoop 4. You have replied by playing your first ball, Blue, between his ball and the peg, so announcing your intention. To make things as difficult as possible for you, your opponent has played his second ball, Yellow, into the second corner. You then shoot at Red and take a bisque (better still, a half-bisque if you have one) if you miss. This is the position shown in fig. 20.

In the following stroke croquet Red to hoop 2 as a pioneer with a normal straight drive. Black should finish close to the Blue provided that you have played Blue into the correct position on your first stroke. Roquet Blue, rushing it a little way towards hoop 1 if possible,

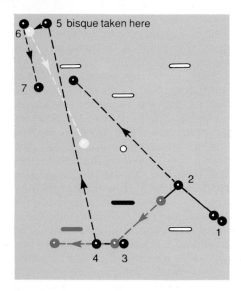

▲ *Fig. 20 'Classic' opening against scratch player: Bab has just taken a bisque (or a half-bisque) and roqueted red*

and then croquet it in position as the pilot for hoop 1. It does not matter where your ball finishes as long as you can play the continuation stroke to somewhere within easy distance of Yellow in the second corner.

You then take a second bisque, roquet Yellow and croquet it to the peg, with Black finishing near Red. Roquet Red, take off to the pilot at hoop 1 and you have set up a perfect four-ball break with the use of two bisques (or $1\frac{1}{2}$ if you used the half-bisque first). Of course, if you manage to hit Red with your first shot, you save a bisque. Note that it does not matter if you hit Yellow when shooting into the second corner; you still have to take a bisque before you can make hoop 1 off Blue.

If general, you should try to get all the balls into good position for the break, but this is not always possible. In order to get the break started, the top priority is to get a good pilot at your next hoop, but that does not mean it has to be done immediately. Obviously, it is easier to croquet a ball into position from a short distance rather than a long one; therefore the ball chosen to be the pilot will normally be the ball closest to the next

hoop – Blue in the above example. The exact position of the pivot is less important than that of the pioneer.

If you have only a few bisques, you cannot afford to spend two of them to set up a break. Instead you should be looking for opportunities to set up a four-ball break with a single bisque. In this way you will get maximum value from the bisques. If you stick in a hoop off your own ball as pilot with a four-ball break set up, you may be tempted to leave the court and hope that your opponent will miss his shot. However, he will certainly shoot with the ball that is your pioneer at your next hoop but one, and your opportunity to maintain a four-ball break with one bisque will vanish.

You should always be on the look-out for chances to make a bisque pay when your opponent has broken down. The balls will nearly always be in court rather than on the yard-line and this could be to your advantage, particularly if one of them is already a pilot or pioneer for you. Get into the habit of thinking what you can do with a bisque each time you step on to the court. You will actually get a double dividend from

this; not only will your own play improve, but you will learn which situations should be avoided when you are giving bisques rather than receiving them.

If you make an error with a hoop approach, leaving your ball in a position where it is impossible to run the hoop, look around to see what you can do with your continuation stroke to make a bisque pay. It is possible, of course, to take position to run the hoop with the continuation stroke and then take the bisque, but there may be better things to do. The pilot is still there by the hoop for you and it may be possible to tidy up the break by using the other balls. For example, where your approach to hoop 3 has gone astray and your pioneer at hoop 4 is out of position, play the continuation stroke to the boundary behind the poor pioneer. Take the bisque and play the pioneer into a better position before returning to the pilot to continue the break.

Intelligent use of bisques will earn you the respect of better players and will lead to a handicap reduction. You will be on the way to becoming a good player yourself.

Doubles play

1 In doubles each player of the side decides which ball he will play with at the start of the game. He must then play with that ball throughout the game.

2 The weaker side receives half a bisque for each unit difference of the combined handicap; e.g. a difference of 4 becomes 2 bisques, a difference of 3 becomes $1\frac{1}{2}$ bisques.

3 One partner can place the balls in a croquet stroke for the other, and each can give the other any advice or help except in actually playing the stroke. (The game is often played with a high-bisquer and a low-bisquer on each side as partners; this can be one of the best ways for a newcomer to learn the tactics of the game.)

4 A good player will play with consideration for his partner, arranging things so that his partner is not required to play strokes beyond his capabilities.

5 Discuss with your partner at the start of every turn what to do, who is to play the turn and how to play it. How-

▲ *'What do I do next, partner?'*

ever, discussion should not be protracted and should take place off the court, particularly if you are double-banking with another game.

6 When your partner is playing his turn, pay attention to his play; you may be able to advise him or prevent him playing by error with the wrong ball.

34

Short croquet

Short croquet was launched as a new variation by the Croquet Association in 1985 to provide a standardised small court game. The court dimensions are 24 yards × 16 yards; a court will fit on a grass tennis court plus surrounds.

The rover hoop is placed 6 yards north of the peg and hoop 5 is 6 yards south of the peg. The four outer hoops are placed 4 yards in from their adjacent boundaries.

The course consists of the first six hoops and the peg (it is thus a 14-point game).

A player is entitled to a lift if the ball he wishes to play has been positioned by the adversary and it is wired from its partner ball (not all other balls). Otherwise, the laws are as for Association Croquet. *See* page 40 for laws.

Beginners usually get a handicap allowance of seven bisques and this is reduced as they become more proficient. The game is played as a full-bisque handicap game, i.e. both players receive their full allowance of bisques.

The tactics should be to set up a four-ball break at the first opportunity, to make five hoops and to leave the court at the end of your turn with all the balls well separated. The opponent should endeavour to do the same. On your next turn use your remaining bisques to set up and play a break with your backward ball. If the bisques last, make all six hoops and attempt to peel your first ball through the rover hoop and peg both out to win. A game played in this attacking way is much quicker (one hour is usually allowed for a game in short croquet tournaments) and more enjoyable than one where bisques are conserved to deal with mistakes.

This is an ideal game for the beginner to learn to play croquet. The smaller dimensions of the court make it easier for a beginner to play a break even when the strokes are not played as accurately as would be desired. Beginners are advised to stay with short croquet until they have mastered the principles of the four-ball break. They will then find the transition to a full-sized court relatively easy and will make progress much more rapidly.

Golf croquet

This is something of a misnomer as the croquet stroke is not used in this game. It is similar to putting in golf, but the aim is to run hoops instead of sinking a ball into a hole. The abbreviated laws are as follows.

1 The opposing sides are Blue and Black against Red and Yellow: doubles or singles can be played.

2 Each side plays alternately and a turn consists of a single stroke only.

3 The balls are played in order of colour: Blue, Red, Black, Yellow. A side has no choice of which ball to play.

4 The course starts from the north baulk-line and the hoops are run from hoop 1 to rover as in Association Croquet. A longer course of eighteen hoops – the last six again after the twelfth – can be played.

5 The side to run the hoop first scores the point, then all balls go on to contest the next hoop. The game ends when one side has scored seven points. (The score is usually kept in the same terms as match-play golf, i.e. number of hoops ahead and number of hoops to play, e.g. two up and three to play.)

6 The peg remains in place but is not used to score a point; if the sides are equal after the last hoop has been run, hoop 3 is contested again to decide the winner.

7 Players are not allowed to strike a ball so that it jumps off the ground.

8 The striker must always play to contest the next hoop in order and must never play solely to gain an advantage for the next hoop but one.

9 To score a point the ball must run the hoop in a single stroke, unless it has previously been sent into the hoop by an adversary.

10 A peeled ball scores the point for itself.

Practice

Any player who wishes to improve his game must practise: an hour spent practising will do more good for your game than many hours spent playing. Failure to practise will lead to stagnation in your play, with countless opportunities lost due to your inability to play good strokes. Practice is inevitably repetitive if it is to be successful and too much repetition can lead to boredom. Give yourself a point each time the stroke is successful and keep a record of your success rate. Set yourself reasonable targets and allow yourself a break from repetitive practice when you achieve them. Keep practice enjoyable and you are more likely to continue with it.

The following routines will help you master the basic strokes.

1 Practise roquets at distances up to 10 yards. Take two sets of balls and start first at a short distance where you are certain to hit all eight shots. Extend the distance to the point where you hit seven out of eight and then to the point where you expect to hit six out of eight. Finish by shooting again at the two shorter distances. Keep a record of your hits and try to beat your target.

2 Practise take-offs from increasing differences to get behind a yard-line ball.

3 Practise hoop approaches from varying distances (up to 4 yards) and angles with the different strokes – stop shots, drives and rolls.

4 Practise hoop running gently to a predetermined spot. Don't try this from greater distances than 1 yard or from extreme angles.

5 Practise straight rushes from hoop 1 to hoop 5, then to hoop 4 and back to hoop 1. Practise cut rushes to the same hoops.

6 Practise straight croquet strokes to put out a pioneer from one hoop to the next hoop but one. Your ball should finish by a target pivot.

7 Practise split croquet strokes from one hoop to the next hoop (your ball) and the next hoop but one (croqueted ball). Start at hoop 4, then hoop 2 and finally hoop 1.

The following routines will help you to master break play. Lay out the break and give yourself an easy hoop approach to start. See how many hoops you can make.

1 Four-ball break from hoop 4. When you can make more than five hoops, try this from hoop 1.

2 Three-ball break from hoop 4. As above, try from hoop 1 when you can make more than five hoops.

3 Two-ball break from hoops 1 to 5 to 4 and back to 1. This is quite difficult for most players.

Bisque taking

Place the opponent balls in tice position and in corner II. Start with your balls joined up on the east boundary. Use bisques to set up a break and to take it to the peg. Don't give up when it is going badly. Keep a record of the number of bisques required. Your handicap should be around twice the average over your last four attempts.

◀ *Jumping a ball through a hoop*

Double-banking

It is often the practice in tournament and club play to *double-bank*, i.e. to play two games simultaneously on the same court, in order to maximise court use. In the second game Green, Brown, Pink and White balls are used. There is surprisingly little interference between the two games, but on occasion a ball from one game has to have its position marked and be removed temporarily from the court in order to give precedence to the other game. Players carry small coins or plastic markers for this purpose. The following customs should be observed in double-banked games.

1   Players should be aware of the course of play in the other game, especially when stepping on to the court at the start of a turn. They should not cross another player's line of aim.

2   Players should not take undue time in play.

3   If one player is making a break, he should normally be given precedence.

4   If two players are approaching the same hoop and both are making breaks, precedence should normally be given to the player most likely to get clear of the hoop first.

5   If two players are approaching the same hoop but neither is making a break, precedence should normally be given to the player who has made the first roquet towards the hoop.

6   Permission should be sought from the players in the other game before a ball is marked. It should not be marked if it is in a critical position near a hoop or the peg, or if it is wired from another ball.

7   A ball which is marked and moved may be left on the court, but should never be placed in a hoop or against the peg.

8   Marked balls should be replaced in their correct positions as soon as possible.

Hints, tips and reminders

1   Stalk the ball before taking up your stance.

2   Keep your head down and your eye on the ball until you have hit it.

3   Think ahead – especially with hoop approaches.

4   Follow through – especially when running hoops and making roquets.

5   Follow through along the line of the swing when playing split croquet strokes.

6   When laying up at the end of your turn, remember the following points:

● put both opponent balls where they will be useful to you in your next turn – not just as far away as possible

● don't leave your balls so that your opponent has a double target with either of his balls

● don't leave either of your opponent balls wired from all others – if this happens, leave your balls well away from both baulk-lines

● if you want to leave a ball by your opponent's hoop, make certain it is the ball for that hoop.

7   When shooting at a ball which is in the middle of the court, always hit hard enough to send your ball off the court.

8   Avoid joining up in mid-court, so giving your opponent a free shot.

9   Concentrate on getting your pioneers in good position when playing a break.

10   If you are several yards away from a ball you want to roquet when playing a break with bisques available, play gently to remain close by the ball if you miss.

11   Look for good opportunities to take bisques – make them pay.

12   When conceding bisques be careful at the end of your turn not to leave a good opportunity for your opponent to use a bisque.

13   Remember you are your own referee when playing – declare any faults you make.

▲ *Refereeing a stroke*

14   Call in a referee or consult your opponent if you are about to play a stroke which could result in fault because you are hampered.

Laws

The main effects of the laws are sum-
marised as follows.

1   The start is from any part of
either baulk-line.

2   You are entitled to a further
stroke after

   (a)   a roquet, after which you
take croquet from the
roqueted ball

   (b)   running your hoop, after
which you play a
continuation stroke

   (c)   a legal croquet stroke, after
which you play a
continuation stroke.

3   At the start of a turn or after
scoring a point by running your
hoop in order you may roquet and
take croquet from each of the other
three balls once only.

4   Your turn ends if during any
stroke except a croquet stroke you
neither

   (a)   make a roquet nor

   (b)   run your next hoop in order.

5   Your turns ends if during a
croquet stroke:

   (a)   the croqueted balls goes off
the court

   (b)   your ball goes off the court,
unless it makes a roquet or
scores its next hoop in order
before leaving the court.

6   Your turns ends if:

   (a)   you do not move or shake
the croqueted ball during a
croquet stroke

   (b)   during any stroke you make
more than one audible
sound between your mallet
and the ball. A second hit on
your ball after making a
roquet is not a fault under
this law

   (c)   you squeeze your ball
between the peg or a hoop
and your mallet – this is a
crush stroke

   (d)   you play with, i.e. strike with
your mallet, a wrong ball.

After the 'faults' (a), (b) and (c) or the
'error' (d) all balls moved as a result of
the fault or error are replaced in their
previous positions.

7   Your turn does not end if:

   (a)   you roquet a ball off the court

   (b)   your ball goes off the court
after it has made a roquet
(when it has become a ball in
hand) or has run its hoop in
order.

8   If any balls are sent into the yard-
line area (*see* exceptions) or off the
court (no exceptions), whether or not
the turn ends, they must be replaced
on the yard-line opposite the point
where they left court or came to rest in
the yard-line area, before the next
stroke.

Exceptions: your ball is not replaced
on the yard-line if it comes to rest in
the yard-line area after running its
hoop in order or after a croquet stroke.
In these cases the ball is played from
where it lies, provided that the turn
has not ended for some other reason.

9   A ball is off the court when any
part of it touches or crosses the vertical
plane from the *inner* edge of the
boundary line.

10   A ball must run its hoop to score
a point. If a ball enters a hoop from the
non-playing side, i.e. in the wrong

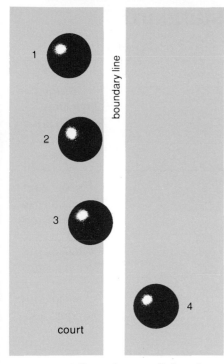

▲ *Fig. 21 Balls in relation to the boundary line: 1 is on the court; 2, 3 and 4 are off the court, although the position of 2 (just touching the vertical plane over the inner edge of the boundary) would be adjudicated by a referee*

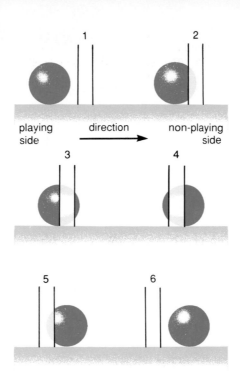

▲ *Fig. 22 Balls in relation to a hoop: 1 and 2 have not started to run the hoop; 3 has started to run the hoop; 4 has not completed the running of the hoop; 5 and 6 have completed the running of the hoop*

direction, it can only score a point subsequently when played in the right direction if it has not already started to run the hoop. A ball has started to run the hoop as soon as it touches a straight edge placed across the non-playing side. A ball has run the hoop when it has come to rest in a position where it cannot be touched by a straight edge placed across the playing-side. (*See* fig. 22.)

11 If at the beginning of his turn a player finds that either of his balls, which has been placed where it is by his opponent, cannot hit the whole of any other ball because either a hoop or the peg is in the way or obstructs his backswing, his ball is wired. He may then lift the wired ball and play it from any position on either baulk-line.

12 A player who takes a bisque must play his bisque turn with the same ball that he was playing immediately before taking the bisque. A player who has said that he will take a bisque may change his mind before playing a stroke: but, if he indicates verbally or by quitting the court that he is not going to take a bisque, then he may not change his mind.

13   During the normal course of the game the players act as their own referees. However, if a position arises where a questionable stroke (e.g. a possible crush or a shot at a ball in a hoop) is about to be played, the striker should consult his opponent before playing the stroke, so that it can be specially watched. When playing a fine take-off, he must be able to say positively that he saw the croqueted ball move. Similarly, when claiming a roquet, he must be able to say positively that his ball touched the other ball.

14   A booklet 'The Laws of Association Croquet' which gives the laws in full is available with other information from The Croquet Association, The Hurlingham Club, Ranelagh Gardens, London SW6 3PR.

Metric equivalents of standard dimensions

	Imperial	*Metric*
Standard court	35 yards	32.0 metres
	28 yards	25.6 metres
	7 yards	6.4 metres
	1 yard	0.9 metres
Peg	18 inches	450 millimetres
	6 inches	150 millimetres
	$1\frac{1}{2}$ inches	38 millimetres
Hoops	12 inches	300 millimetres
	$3\frac{3}{4}$ inches	95 millimetres
Balls	$3\frac{5}{8}$ inches	92 millimetres
	16 ounces	454 grammes

Advanced level play

Croquet may seem at times a frustratingly difficult game for the beginner but, once the basic skills have been mastered, it is possible to manoeuvre the balls around the court with a great deal of precision. One of the best ways for a novice player to begin to appreciate the subtleties of croquet is to watch expert players in action. However, there are differences between the game played on handicap at club level and that played on level terms at major championships.

Good players can easily make an all-round break of twelve hoops in a single turn and the best players became adept at making such a break and leaving the position shown in fig. 23 where the player's balls are joined up close to the third corner and those of the opponent are cross-wired at hoop 1. The opponent was left with a shot of some 35 yards and one which he could rarely expect to hit. The shot had to be taken because

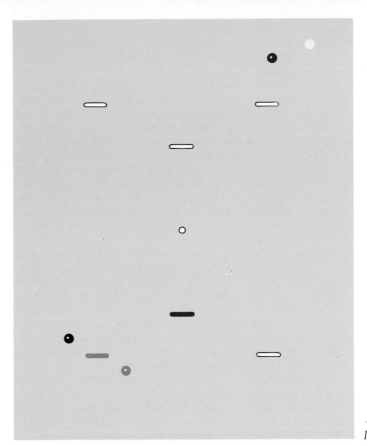

◄ *Fig. 23 Wired leave at hoop 1*

43

there was no safe position to play either ball; with a pioneer at hoop 1 and a rush to hoop 2 it was not difficult for the first player to make a second all-round break and finish the game. At the top level croquet became a one-sided game; the first player to make a break would almost invariably win.

The laws of the game were extended to give a fairer chance to the out-player by allowing him to lift either ball and play it from either baulk-line, so reducing the length of the shot at the end of the first break, or allowing him in special circumstances to take an immediate contact. This in turn has induced good players to attempt further feats of skill.

Under advanced play laws a player is entitled to a lift if his opponent has run 1-back or 4-back with his ball in the preceding turn; he is entitled to a contact, i.e. he may start his turn by placing either of his balls in contact with any other ball to take croquet, if his opponent has run both 1-back and 4-back in the preceding turn with a ball before its partner ball has made 1-back. A player has therefore potentially four lift shots or a contact and two lift shots during

the course of a game.

Players usually prefer not to concede the contact and so give up the innings. Instead, they will take their first break as far as, but not through, 4-back, i.e. making only the first nine hoops, and finish their turn with a lift leave. Some examples of lift leaves are shown in figs 24 a,b and c. In each case Ray has played his turn with Red. Because Ray has run 1-back with Red, Bab now has the option to lift either Black or Blue and play it from anywhere on either baulk-line. Her shot is reduced to some 14 to 17 yards with a much greater probability of hitting.

If Bab misses the shot, Ray will play Yellow and try to take his next break to the peg. Although in so doing he will run 1-back and 4-back in the same turn, he will not concede a contact because his partner ball has already made 1-back, but he will concede a lift. Bab therefore has a further chance with a reduced length shot.

If Ray can then take his backward ball (Red) to the peg and finish the game with a peg-out he will have conceded only two out of potentially four lifts during the game. One lift was saved

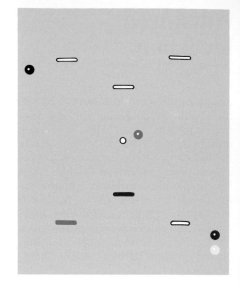

▲ *Fig. 24a Old standard leave*

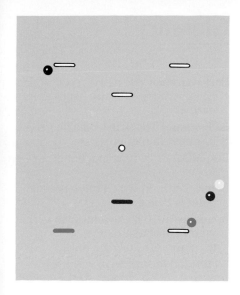

▲ *Fig. 24b New standard leave*

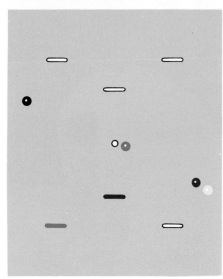

▲ *Fig. 24c Diagonal spread*

because he ran 1-back and 4-back with his second ball in the same turn, and the other because he finished the game before Bab could take her last lift after Yellow ran 4-back.

If Ray is an expert player, there are further interesting possibilities open to him. The lift is only conceded if 1-back or 4-back is made with the striker's ball. The partner ball may be peeled through either of these hoops without penalty. After one of the lift leaves shown in fig. 24, Ray will attempt to take Yellow to the peg, peeling Red through its last three hoops, and peg both balls out to finish the game. This feat is known as a triple peel and is the hallmark of the expert player and the aspiration of most lesser players.

The mechanics of the triple peel are beyond the scope of this book, but it is a delight to see an expert playing with the precision required to get the partner ball into a peeling position.

It is possible to perform more than three peels in a single turn but the opportunity usually only occurs when the player has failed to take his first ball to 4-back. However, there is one exception to this: the sextuple peel. Top players will occasionally make the first six hoops and end their turn with a leave. Then, if the shot is missed, they will attempt to take their backward ball to the peg, peeling the partner ball through its last six hoops on the way, and peg both balls out.

Glossary

Backward ball The ball of a side which has not made as many hoops as its partner

Ball in hand The striker's ball when it has made a roquet

Bisque An extra turn in a handicap game

Break A turn in which more than one point is scored

Break down To make a mistake so that your turn comes to an end involuntarily during a break

Continuation stroke An extra stroke played after a croquet stroke or after running a hoop

Croquet To strike your ball which has been placed in contact with another, so that they both move

Croqueted ball The ball from which croquet has been taken

Double tap A fault in which more than one audible sound is made on striking the ball

Drive A natural croquet stroke played with normal follow-through

Free shot An opportunity to shoot at a ball or balls which gives no advantage to the opponent if the shot is missed

Forward ball The ball of a side which has made more hoops than the other

Hit in To make a roquet when you are the out-player

In-player The player who has the innings and thereby the advantage

Lift To lift your ball from where it lies and play it from a baulk-line

Out-player The player without the innings

Peel To send a ball other than your own through its next hoop in order

Peg out To make a rover ball hit the peg and thus be removed from the game

Penult The penultimate hoop or the last hoop but one

Pilot ball The ball off which you make a hoop

Pioneer ball The ball which is waiting at your next hoop but one

Pivot ball The auxiliary ball in a four-ball break

Playing side The side from which a ball enters a hoop in order to run it

Roll A croquet stroke played in such a way as to increase the distance travelled by the striker's ball relative to the croqueted ball

Roquet To make your ball hit another

Rover A ball which has made all its hoops and may be pegged out or may peg out other rovers. Also, the last hoop

Rush To roquet a ball to a predetermined position

Rush line Continuation in both directions of the line of the proposed rush

Split A croquet stroke in which the balls go in different directions

Stop shot A croquet stroke played in such a way as to decrease the distance travelled by the striker's ball relative to the croqueted ball

Take off A croquet stroke which sends the striker's ball to a predetermined position and moves the croqueted ball by a relatively small amount

Tice A ball played to a position, usually from a baulk-line, which is intended to entice the opponent to shoot at it

Triple peel A turn in which the player peels another ball through its last three hoops and pegs it out

Wired A ball is wired if a hoop or the peg obscures the direct line of the striker's ball to any part of it or if a hoop or the peg interferes with the normal swing of the mallet

Index